YOUR LAND
AND
MY LAND
The Middle East

We Visit

IRAN

Pete

DiPrimio

Mitchell Lane
PUBLISHERS
P.O. Box 196
Hockessin, Delaware 19707

YOUR LAND AND MY LAND
The Middle East

Afghanistan
Iran
Iraq
Israel
Kuwait
Oman
Pakistan
Saudi Arabia
Turkey
Yemen

YOUR LAND
AND
MY LAND
The Middle East

We Visit

IRAN

Mitchell Lane
PUBLISHERS

Printing   1   2   3   4   5   6   7   8   9

Special thanks to Indiana businessman Nasir Jallal for his personal insights into Iran, and for the fabulous cup of tea he shared with me. Mr. Jallal grew up in Kabul, Afghanistan, and now lives in Bloomington, Indiana.

Library of Congress Cataloging-in-Publication Data
DiPrimio, Pete.
  We visit Iran / by Pete DiPrimio.
      p. cm. — (Your land and my land: the Middle East)
  Includes bibliographical references and index.
  ISBN 978-1-58415-954-4 (library bound)
  1. Iran—Juvenile literature. I. Title.
  DS254.75.D57 2011
  955—dc22
                                                                    2011016765

eBook ISBN: 9781612280998

PUBLISHER'S NOTE: This story is based on the author's extensive research, which he believes to be accurate. Documentation of this research is on page 61.

The Internet sites referenced herein were active as of the publication date. Due to the fleeting nature of some web sites, we cannot guarantee they will all be active when you are reading this book.

To reflect current usage, we have chosen to use the secular era designations BCE ("before the common era") and CE ("of the common era") instead of the traditional designations BC ("before Christ") and AD (*anno Domini,* "in the year of the Lord").

Contents

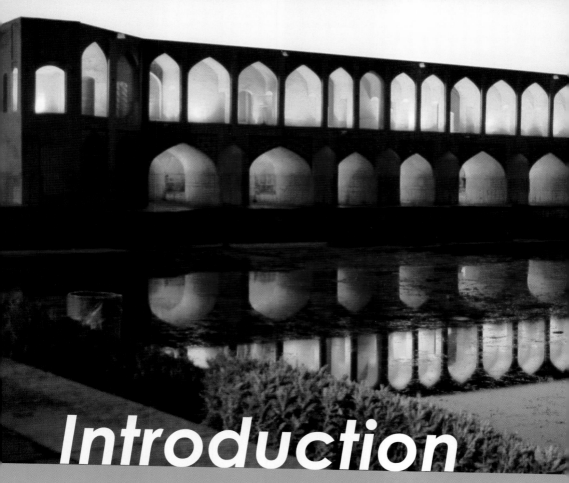

Introduction

Iran is a Middle Eastern country of contrasts. Harsh, unforgiving deserts give way to snowy mountains that soar to more than 18,000 feet (5,500 meters). The sparkling waters of the Persian Gulf, Caspian Sea, and Gulf of Oman are offset by salt deserts, marshes, and even rain forests.[1] Elected presidents obey unelected, powerful religious leaders. Modern cities coexist with spectacular ruins from one of the world's greatest ancient empires.[2] Persians (whose ancestors are Europeans) make up the largest group of people, while Arabs are just a small part of the population. The first Iranian astronaut was a woman, even though Iran is a country that treats its women very strictly.[3]

Iran has kept its ancient language alive and follows a strict Shi'ite interpretation of Islam. The country is rich in oil, but international concern over its nuclear energy ambitions has created tension and worries about war. Its 31 provinces contain bustling bazaars that offer some of the best and most expensive carpets in the world.

Khaju Bridge, built in 1650 CE, spans the Zayandeh River in the Iranian province of Isfahan. The 345-foot- (105-meter-) long structure is also used as a dam, helping to control water flow and irrigate nearby gardens. Public meetings were once held there.

The Middle East extends from southwest Asia to southeastern Europe and northeastern Africa. It is the cradle of civilization and the birthplace of three major religions—Islam, Christianity, and Judaism.[4] Its abundance of oil gives it huge geographical and political importance. While relationships between Middle Eastern countries are often strained, Iran's potential to be the dominant power in the region makes it a nation to be reckoned with.

The Jameh Mosque in the city of Tabriz is located near the city's Grand Bazaar and Constitutional House.

Welcome to Iran

While Iran is an Islamic nation, it is not an Arab one, which makes it unique in the Middle East. Its first great conquering people were Aryan tribes that came out of Eastern Europe. Iranians have their own language, called Persian or Farsi, while the rest of the Arab world speaks mostly Arabic.

It is a land of great beauty, from its mountains and deserts to its historical sites. It is rich in oil and also in art and poetry, some of which is over a thousand years old.[1]

Iran is bordered by the Caspian Sea to the north, then clockwise by Turkmenistan, Afghanistan, Pakistan, the Gulf of Oman, the Persian Gulf, Iraq, Turkey, and Azerbaijan. A tiny tip of Armenia also touches Iran. Few people can live in Iran's harsh, desert-like interior, which is part of the Iranian Plateau. Instead, people have settled in the mountainous regions of western and eastern Iran.

Tehran, the capital, is a modern city with well-preserved historical roots. There's a great view from the famous Shahid Motahari Mosque with its eight minarets (tall, slender towers). The city has one of the world's biggest bazaars (a type of shopping center), and museums that display pottery, paintings, archaeological finds, and carpets (one carpet is 450 years old). It has a zoo, theater, national library, and university.[2]

Iran was once called Persia. Under its king Cyrus the Great, Persia grew into a vast empire that stretched from the Indus River to the Mediterranean and from the Caucasus Mountains to the Indian Ocean.

The Milad Tower in Tehran is the tallest tower in Iran and one of the tallest in the world. It is 1,427 feet (435 meters) high.

Later, Egypt also became part of the empire. Persia was conquered by a succession of invaders, including Alexander the Great. Eventually the Muslim Arabs, strong followers of Islam, conquered Persia in the name of God (or Allah). They roared in from what is now Iraq in the seventh century and changed Iranian history forever.

Iran has become a culture of strict religious law. While it offers stunning scenery and a rich history, it is a dangerous place for tourists and for those who disagree with its government.

At the end of 2010, diplomatic cables that were supposed to stay secret were leaked over the Internet. Dubbed WikiLeaks, the controversial papers ruffled international feathers while exposing some troubling events. One WikiLeaks story tells of a 75-year-old Iranian dentist, Hossein Ghanbarzadeh Vahedi, who left Iran during the 1979 Islamic revolution.[3] He moved to Los Angeles and became an American citizen, but he missed his homeland. He wanted to visit his parents' graves, so he did in May of 2008. When he tried to return to the United States, Iranian authorities would not let him. They arrested him and took his passport. According to the cables, they said they would release him if he paid a $150,000 fine and if he promised to convince his sons, who worked as music industry executives in Los Angeles, to stop promoting musicians and singers the government considered "antiregime."

Vahedi said the pop singers sometimes fired up crowds in Iran by criticizing the government. In the United States, people have the right to criticize leaders and dress daringly, but in Iran they do not. Musical performances sometimes included female dancers wearing costumes Iranian authorities considered "immoral," Vahedi said.

The dentist decided to escape. He paid two guides US$5,000 to lead him over a dangerous, cold mountain pass on horseback. The fourteen-hour trip was so frigid and draining that at one point he fell off the horse and thought he was "going to die by freezing to death on a mountainside." The guides had to hug him to keep him warm. Vahedi finally crossed the border into Turkey. He paid another US$2,500 for a place to stay, food, and a ride to a bus station. He took a 10-hour bus ride to Ankara, Turkey, where he showed up at the U.S. Embassy. Those officials helped him get back to the United States.[4]

Unlike the United States, Iranian government officials keep tight control of their citizens. Calls for reform have been squashed since the 1979 revolution that put religious leaders in power. Not even the 2009 election, which many Iranians believed was fixed, or the Arab Spring of 2011, when demands for reform erupted in many Middle Eastern countries, changed the government. Its control was too strong.[5]

Where in the World ◎

WHERE IN THE WORLD IS IRAN?

ISLAMIC REPUB
IRA

Legend	
◎	National capital
⊙	Provincial capital
○	City, town
✈	Airport
–··–··–	International boundary
–·–·–·	Provincial boundary
——	Main road
——	Secondary road
+++	Railroad

The boundaries and names shown and the designations
used on this map do not imply official endorsement or
acceptance by the United Nations.

ISLAMIC REP. OF
IRAN

IRAN FACTS AT A GLANCE

Full name: Islamic Republic of Iran

Language: Persian and Persian (Farsi) dialects (58 percent), Turkic and Turkic dialects (26 percent), Kurdish (9 percent), Luri (2 percent), Balochi (1 percent), Arabic (1 percent), Turkish (1 percent), other (2 percent)

Population: 76,923,300 (July 2010 est.)

Land area: 636,296 square miles (1,648,195 square kilometers); roughly the size of Alaska

Capital: Tehran

Government: Islamic Republic

Ethnic makeup: Persian (51 percent), Azeri (24 percent), Gilaki and Mazandarani (8 percent), Kurd (7 percent), Arab (3 percent), Lur (2 percent), Baloch (2 percent), Turkmen (2 percent)

Religions: Muslim (98 percent, with 89 percent Shia and the rest Sunni), other: Zoroastrian, Jewish, Christian, and Baha'i

Exports: Petroleum (80 percent), chemical and petrochemical products, fruits and nuts, carpets

Imports: Industrial raw materials and intermediate goods, capital goods, foodstuffs and other consumer goods, technical services

Crops: Wheat, rice, other grains, sugar beets, sugarcane, fruits, nuts, cotton, dairy products, wool, caviar

Average temperatures: August: 71–96°F (22–36°C); January 30–40°F (−1–8°C)

Average rainfall: 9.8 inches (25 centimeters)

Highest point: Kuh-e Damavand—18,606 feet (5,671 meters) high

Longest river: Safid River—600 miles (1,000 kilometers) long

Flag: Three equal horizontal bands of green (top), white, and red; the national emblem (a stylized representation of the word Allah in the shape of a tulip, a symbol of martyrdom) in red is centered in the white band; Allah Akbar (God is great) in white Arabic script is repeated 11 times along the bottom edge of the green band and 11 times along the top edge of the red band; green is the color of Islam and also represents growth, white symbolizes honesty and peace, and red stands for bravery and martyrdom

National flower: Red rose (*Rosa*)

Source: CIA—*The World Factbook:* "Iran"

 The tomb of Cyrus the Great still stands more than 2,500 years after it was built.

Chapter 2

History of Iran

Cyrus was a baby when he first scared a great ruler.

Astyages was the king of Media in what is now eastern Iran about 2,500 years ago. He was descended from a group of people from Eastern Europe and Russia called the Aryans who had arrived in the area around 1600 BCE. According to legend, he had a dream about his daughter, Mandane. A great vine grew from her loins and covered all of Asia. He asked his priests what the dream meant. They said his daughter would have a son who would conquer Media, then all the lands around it. That son turned out to be Cyrus.[1]

Although Astyages first tried to have his grandson killed, he allowed the boy to return to Mandane and his father, Cambyses, king of the small Achaemenid Empire that was part of Media. Cyrus grew up in traditional Persian fashion, which was to "ride a horse, draw a bow and speak the truth."[2] He learned to fight on foot as well as horseback and took survival training in the wilderness. He finally replaced his father in 559 BCE and quickly unified the tribes of Persia.

Worried, Astyages sent an army to defeat his grandson in 550 BCE. The Median army, however, decided to join Cyrus. Astyages was captured by his own generals. At the time, most defeated kings were killed, usually by beheading. Instead, Cyrus let his grandfather live but stripped him of all titles and powers.

That generosity in victory became commonplace under Cyrus, whose Persian Empire included what is now Iran, Turkey, Israel, Saudi Arabia, Pakistan, Kazakhstan, and Krygyzstan. He respected different cultures and people. As long as they understood who was in charge and paid tribute, he left them alone.

Cyrus lost only one battle, but it cost him his life. In 530 BCE, he was getting ready to invade and conquer Egypt when a nomad tribe on the northeastern border of the empire, between the Caspian Sea and the Aral Sea, attacked. Cyrus was killed, along with most of his men. His body was taken back to Pasargadae, the site of his first great victory, and buried there in a mausoleum that still stands.

The empire soon expanded under another great leader, Darius I, to include parts of what are now Greece and Egypt, and even the Indus River near what is now India. It was eventually conquered by the Macedonian general Alexander the Great around 331 BCE. Other invaders followed, including the Parthians, the Romans, and the Sassanians. Finally, in 640 CE, the Arabs conquered Persia as the Islamic religion came to dominate the Middle East and the Mediterranean Sea area.

The Turks later conquered Persia. In the 1380s, a great general swept in from Mongolia. Called Timur, now better known as Tamerlane, he built a large empire that included parts of Iraq, Syria, and Turkey.

The Safavid dynasty took control at the beginning of the sixteenth century. In 1727, another powerful leader, Ardir Shah, took charge. One of the last great conquerors of Asia, he would rule until 1747. In the early 1800s, the Russians arrived to dominate the area. Oil was discovered in the region in 1908, and that drew the interest of the British. Russia and Great Britain battled for control. Both occupied Persia during World War I, but they withdrew after the war. A Persian officer, Reza Khan, became the leader, first as prime minister, then, in 1925, as king. In 1935, Reza Khan changed the country's name from Persia to Iran to memorialize the Aryan tribes who had conquered the area in ancient times. He wanted to show that Iran was tied to Europe.

Reza Khan ruled until 1941, when the Soviet Union and Great Britain took control again. Both countries wanted the oil the area produced for their military during World War II. They both withdrew in 1946, and Reza Khan's son, Reza Pahlavi, took charge. There were

Mohammad Reza Pahlavi ruled as the shah of Iran. He replaced his father, Reza Khan, in 1941, but did not take full control of the country until the early 1960s. He became very unpopular because of his harsh rule and fled the country in 1979. He died a year later.

hopes the country would become a constitutional monarchy or even a democracy. But in 1951, when Prime Minister Mohammad Mosaddeq pushed to nationalize the British-owned oil industry, the British and the United States got upset. They eventually supported a takeover that forced Mosaddeq from office and gave all the power to the shah.[3]

That was the end of hopes for democracy. The shah ruled for the next 25 years, but change was coming.

Ruhollah Musavi Khomeini was a great Islamic leader and the inspiration for the 1979 revolution. In 1962 he was recognized as one of six grand ayatollah (most important religious leaders) in Iranian Shi'ite Islam.

Chapter

3

Supreme Leader, Government of Faith

As a powerful Muslim religious leader, called an ayatollah, Ruhollah Musavi Khomeini had spent fifteen years exiled from Iran because he disagreed with the government and wanted change. Khomeini believed the ruler of Iran, the shah, was too close to the United States and had lost touch with the Islamic faith, particularly the Shi'ite branch that dominated the country. He saw the government as corrupt, spending too much money on things other than helping the people.[1]

Fearing an overthrow, the shah kicked Khomeini out of the country in 1964. Khomeini lived much of his exile in neighboring Iraq, where he talked about someday returning to form an Islamic republic in Iran that would combine politics and religion into one government. It would follow the conservative Shi'ite style based on the strict teachings of the Prophet Muhammad, the founder of Islam. Even though Khomeini no longer lived in Iran, his words were very influential. The people became angry and pushed for a revolution that would overthrow the shah.

Khomeini was born into a religious family that claimed it was descended from the Prophet Muhammad. This was important because Shi'ites believe only descendants of Mohammad can become religious leaders. Khomeini's father was murdered when he was five months old, and he was raised by his mother and an aunt. At six years old he started studying the Koran, Islam's holy book. At age fifteen, his mother and aunt died, and he gave himself to religion and the people.

The shah fled the country in late January of 1979 because of massive protests and the loss of the army's support. Two weeks later, Khomeini finally returned to Iran. Nearly 3 million people came to cheer and see him. He promised to create a government that was ruled by religious leaders first, then politicians. The Western world, particularly the United States, did not know what to think.[2]

A few months after Khomeini's return, the shah became seriously ill with cancer and went to the United States to get medical care.[3] Supporters of Khomeini saw this as a chance to make changes in their government. A group of student supporters of Khomeini captured the U.S. embassy in Tehran and took 63 Americans hostage. Thirteen were released within two weeks. The rest were held captive for more than a year. The students said they would release the hostages if the United States turned over the shah for crimes against the nation. President Jimmy Carter said he would not hand over the shah, so Iran kept the hostages. When the shah died in Egypt in 1980 and Iraq invaded Iran that same year (the start of an eight-year war between the two countries), Iranian officials began talking to the United States about releasing the hostages. They were finally released just as Ronald Reagan became U.S. president in January 1981—after 444 days of captivity.

Meanwhile, in April 1979, Khomeini and other religious leaders created the Islamic Republic of Iran. Keeping his promise, the new government allowed some politicians to be elected by the people while ensuring that religious leaders would have a big say in laws and culture.

The new government gave final political power to a wise religious scholar, called the supreme leader, who would be appointed for life, although he could be fired by religious leaders.[4] The first supreme leader was Ayatollah Khomeini, who ruled until his death at age 89 in 1989.

In June of that year, Ali Hosseini Khamenei became the supreme leader. He answered only to the Assembly of Experts, a group of 86 clerics (religious leaders) elected by the people.

Like the United States, Iran has three branches of government: the executive, the legislative, and the judicial branch.[5]

American hostages celebrate their release in January of 1981 after 444 days in captivity.

The executive branch is led by the supreme leader, and then the president. The president is elected by the people. He can serve two straight four-year terms, plus another as long as it is not consecutive. Mahmoud Ahmadinejad became president in August of 2005 and was reelected in 2009. His vice president for the second term was Mohammad Reza Rahimi.

The president chooses a council of ministers, which has to be approved by the legislature. The supreme leader also has influence in these appointments.

The executive branch has three main oversight organizations. The first is the Assembly of Experts (Majles-Khobregan). This elected group picks the supreme leader, reviews his performance, and fires him if necessary.

First Vice President Mohammad Reza Rahimi took office on September 13, 2009. The First Vice President is the most important of Iran's 12 vice presidents.

The second is the Expediency Council (Majma-e-Tashkhis-e-Maslahat-e Nezam), which has power over all three branches. It settles government disputes, advises national religious leaders, and supervises the entire government.

The third is the Council of Guardians of the Constitution (Shora-ye Negban-e Qanon-e Asas-si), which determines whether laws are constitutional and faithful to Islamic law, makes sure candidates are suitable for public office, and runs the national elections. It can disqualify candidates, and sometimes does so as a way to control election results.

The judicial branch has a supreme court (Qeveh Qazaieh) and a four-member High Council of the Judiciary. Led by the same judge, the Court and High Council make sure all laws are enforced. Lower courts include a clerical court, a revolutionary court, and an administrative court.

The legislative branch, called the Islamic Consultative Assembly, or Majles-e-Shura-ye-Eslami, has 290 members who are elected to four-year terms. The main political parties are the conservatives (also called Islamics), the reformers (who favor less strict social laws), the independents, and the religious minorities.

Political parties are often groups who come together before elections and then break up afterward. The Islamic Iran Participation Front (IIPF) is one of the largest groups. There also are political pressure groups that aren't parties, but support certain leaders and either reform or conservative parties.

Mahmoud Ahmadinejad became the sixth president of Iran in 2005.[6] He had earned his PhD in traffic and transport from Tehran's University of Science and Technology and became mayor of Tehran in 2003. As mayor he cut back on social freedoms and got rid of the reforms that earlier mayors had put in place. Favoring strict Islamic laws, he criticized the United States and Israel. He angered people by saying the Jewish Holocaust (the murder of millions of Jews by German Nazis during World War II) was a "myth," and that he saw a day when a Palestinian country would replace Israel.

Anger grew when Ahmadinejad was reelected in the disputed election of June 2009. He won with 62.6 percent of the vote. Main challenger Mir Hussein Moussavi Khamenei got 33.8 percent.[7] Protesters claimed there was cheating and fraud—in 50 cities, there were more votes cast than the number of registered voters—but the results were allowed to stand. Tensions increased when Ahmadinejad violently suppressed those who opposed him. More than 30 people were killed and more than a thousand were arrested. Iranian officials said other countries, mostly Great Britain, stirred up the protesters. In February 2011, Moussavi and another presidential challenger, Mehdi Karroubi, were put under extreme house arrest. After their supporters fought with security forces, some Iranian officials said Moussavi and Karroubi should be executed.[8]

Mount Damavand is the highest volcano in the Middle East. While it hasn't erupted in recorded history, it has shown some volcanic activity, making it dormant rather than extinct. It is popular for hiking and skiing.

Chapter 4

A Land to Explore

At 18,606 feet (5,671 meters) tall, Mount Damavand is the highest mountain in Iran. Wind blasts across its rocky surface at up to 90 miles (150 kilometers) per hour. Near the peak, it is always so cold that the snow never melts. People have hiked and explored the mountain for more than 5,000 years. It and the surrounding areas continue to be popular hiking, climbing, and skiing destinations.[1]

There are many legends about the mountain. In one of the most famous stories, invaders called the Turans had captured the northern part of what is now Iran. It was a hard place to rule, so they made an offer to the conquered Persians. The Turans would redraw the border between Persia and Turan at a distance from Mt. Damavand. The distance would be determined by how far a Persian could shoot an arrow from the top of the mountain. The Persians agreed. They built a special bow and arrow and gave it to Arash, a great Persian archer. He fired an arrow deep into Turan (one story said the arrow traveled the distance of a 40-day walk; others said it traveled from dawn to noon, or even dawn to dusk). Persia gained more land than it had lost to the invaders.[2]

Arash the Archer

Mount Damavand is part of the Alborz (also spelled Elburz) Mountain Range that borders the Caspian Sea in northern Iran. It is a young volcano that has formed over the last 10,000 years. Hot springs on the sides of the mountain and steam vents (called fumaroles) at the summit tell scientists it is dormant, but not extinct, so it could erupt someday.

Near the top is Sulfur Hill (Dood Kooh), formed by volcanic activity. It is covered with sulfur stones. In the summer, when the sun shines on the stones, sulfur gas rises, irritating the eyes and throat and smelling like rotten eggs.

Wolves, foxes, and jackals live in the range at altitudes of up to nearly 13,000 feet (4,000 meters). Bears live in the northern forests but rarely move above the timberline. Goats, sheep, boars, rabbits, eagles, and gazelles can be seen at nearly 16,000 feet (5,000 meters) in the summer.

The weather in Iran is dry and hot in the summer, harsh and cold in the winter. Generally warm-weather clothing is worn in the summer (usually April to October) and medium-weight jackets in the winter (November to March). In the plains there isn't a lot of rain, but the area around Mount Damavand gets 55 inches (140 centimenters) of rain a year.

The Alborz Mountains are only about 30 miles (48 kilometers) northeast of Tehran. People can ski in the winter at resorts such as Abe Ali, the Noor Slope, and Shemshak. Cable cars carry travelers to the peaks. Tourist towns Rey, Varamin, and Qazvin are also popular.[3]

Water skiing is available at the Karaj River near Tehran. Many streams and rivers are well stocked with trout. The Karaj River and the Sefid Rud (River) also are full of fish. The Sefid Rud meanders down from its beginning in the Kurdistan Mountains for around 600 miles (1,000 kilometers), helping to keep the Gilan Plain fertile. Trout is also found in Haraz, a 90-mile- (145-kilometer-) long river that irrigates the Mazandaran province before reaching the Caspian Sea.[4] Along the Caspian shore, in the northern part of the country, there are thick rain forests, where Persian ironwood, Persian silk trees, and Oriental beech trees grow.

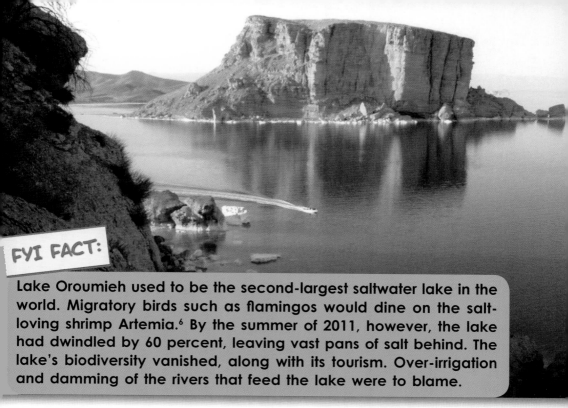

On the other side of the country are the Zagros Mountains, which separate Iran from Iraq. In this home of the endangered Persian leopard, many of the peaks are higher than 9,000 feet (2,750 meters). The highest is Zard Kuh at 14,921 feet (4,550 meters).

The center and eastern parts of the country are mostly barren, rolling desert, although Iranians have built irrigation canals called qanats. There also are green oases where there is enough water for plants such as vines, date palms, and myrtle to live. The Persian Gulf coastal areas showcase limestone cliffs and plenty of sand, providing lots of opportunity for water sports.[5]

Religion is crucial in Iranians' daily lives. Muslims pray five times a day. Men are also required to perform Friday prayers, while women can if they want.

Iran has more people than any other Persian Gulf country—about 77 million in 2010. Nearly 22 percent (a little more than 14 million) are under 15 years old. The average age is 26.3 years. About 68 percent of the population lives in cities.

About 51 percent of the people are Persian, with another 24 percent Azeri, who live in the northwestern part of the country. Only 3 percent are Arab. Just over half the population—58 percent—speaks Persian (Farsi), 26 percent speak a Turkish dialect, and 9 percent speak Kurdish. Only 1 percent speaks Arabic.

Even though Iran is not an Arab country, it is a Muslim one, with 98 percent following the Islamic faith. Of those, 89 percent are Shia (also Shi'ite) and 9 percent are Sunni. The rest of the religions are divided between Christian, Jewish, Zoroastrian (an ancient Persian religion that also believes in one god), and Baha'i.[1]

Iranians overall are very friendly and like to entertain. It is common for them to offer tea. Guests are expected to accept.

Most Iranians eat meals with a spoon and a fork. Visitors who choose a Western dish can eat with a knife and a fork.[2] Islamic law forbids eating pork (and drinking alcohol), but there are plenty of other fantastic food choices.

Iranian cuisine often includes cauliflower, eggplant, tomatoes, spinach, beans, and lentils; and lamb, mutton (sheep), chicken, and beef.[3] Rice is in almost everything. Some of the more popular rice dishes are *adass polo* (lentil rice), *baghali polo* (lime bean rice), *chelo sefeed* (white rice), *haveeg polo* (carrot rice), and even *sabzi polo* (vegetable rice). Rice is eaten with wheat bread, yogurt (often home-made), and lamb.

Stews are another staple. There is *khoresht resenjan* (chicken with pomegranate sauce stew), *khoresht bamieh* (okra stew), *khoresht ghormeh* (green vegetable stew), and *abgousht* (beef stew). Stews are often fla-vored with cinnamon, cloves, turmeric, cardamom, saffron, garlic, and lime.

**Ash-e anar
Pomegranate soup**

For the main course there's *mahi sefeed,* which is white fish. How about some *kabab kubideh,* which is grilled meat such as beef or lamb? If you like soufflés, try *kookoo sabzi* (vegetable soufflé). *Haleem* is wheat pud-ding that includes stew meat.

For desert, try *rangeenak halva.* This combination of fresh dates, white powdered sugar, shelled walnuts, cinnamon, and sesame seeds is baked for just a few minutes to get everything to stick together.

Fruit and vegetable juices are popular beverages, as are sparkling min-eral water, tea (often sipped in teahouses called *ghahye khane*), and *doogh* (a cold drink made from yogurt and mineral water).

**Iranian cookies
with raisins:
Shirini keshmeshi**

Iranian officials want to control what people can do, see, and hear. More than 80 percent of the population watches TV, mostly the government-run stations such as the Islamic Republic of Iran Broadcasting (IRIB).[4] There are eight national channels, one news channel, about 30 province channels, and some international channels. The most popular channel is the

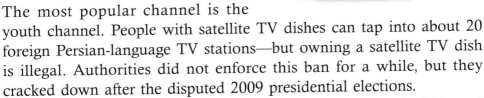

Tea set

youth channel. People with satellite TV dishes can tap into about 20 foreign Persian-language TV stations—but owning a satellite TV dish is illegal. Authorities did not enforce this ban for a while, but they cracked down after the disputed 2009 presidential elections.

There were 32.2 million Internet users at the end of 2009, and probably more than 40 million by the end of 2010. That's more than half the population. However, the government does not allow Iranians to use social networking sites like Facebook. The people also can't go on Twitter, so tweeting is out. Forget about watching YouTube videos. They are all blocked.

Political and human rights web sites are also blocked. Bloggers and online activists unhappy with the government have been arrested. Even foreign broadcasters have trouble. BBC Persian TV (part of the British Broadcasting Corporation) had its satellite broadcasts blocked following the disputed elections in 2009. Hundreds of journalists were arrested for publishing articles critical of the election, including Iranian journalist Ahmad Zeidabadi.[5] He was charged with plotting to overthrow the government with a "soft revolution." He was sentenced to six years in prison and five years internal exile, and banned for life from working as a journalist. In the spring of 2011, while still in prison, he received the United Nation's World Press Freedom Award.

Government control and religious law determine what is and isn't proper, especially when it comes to women. Men are allowed up to four wives. Women can have only one husband. Women also aren't allowed to watch soccer matches in Iranian stadiums. Men are.[6]

Men can wear pretty much whatever they want—jeans, khakis, T-shirts, dress shirts, casual shirts, and business suits. Women can do the same thing—in the privacy of their home. Outside they have to follow a strict Islamic dress code called the hijab laws or risk getting in trouble.[7] Women can either wear a robe that covers them from head to toe, called a chador, or wear a long coat called a manteau. If they wear the manteau they also have to wear pants, thick socks, and a scarf (*maghnew*) that covers most if not all of their hair. They cannot wear makeup.

Qashqai nomad woman

Iranian women used to be able to dress more like women in the United States do, but that changed after the 1979 Islamic revolution. The hijab laws were passed in 1981.

Overall, customs that are considered Western, particularly those from the United States, are not acceptable. Members of the opposite sex may not shake hands. It is illegal for non-Muslim men to date or marry Muslim women. Those who break the law can go to jail.

Some people like the discipline and structure that such Islamic laws provide. Others find it repressive and harmful. They push for change, and peacefully protest by wearing green. The green item might be a shirt, wristband, tie, scarf, or even a little ribbon.

Massoumeh Ebtekar is an Iranian scientist and politician who first gained fame as the spokesperson for the students who occupied the U.S. Embassy in 1979 during the hostage crisis. From 1997 to 2005 she was the vice president of Iran, the first woman to hold such a high government position. She supports the "Green Wave" movement. In 2009, she wrote: "Green is the buzz word today. It is the color specifically chosen by supporters of Mir Hossein [Moussavi]. In Iranian culture as well as Islamic tradition green is the most meaningful color. Now, green is taken as a sign of support for change, a sign of opposition to current government policies and as a sign of choosing [Moussavi]. Green head bands, green T-shirts, green scarves are the political fashion in Iran today."[8]

Thousands of supporters of presidential challenger Moussavi (circled) gathered in the capital city of Tehran in June 2009 to protest his election loss. His supporters continue to wear green.

Islam was founded by the Prophet Muhammad, who was born in the city of Mecca in what is now Saudi Arabia in 570 CE. At that time, Arabs believed in about 360 gods and goddesses. When Muhammad was forty, the angel Gabriel came to him. Muhammad wrote down their talks into what is now called the Koran, the Islamic holy book. Gabriel said that Arabs should worship one god—Allah. Muslims believe that Adam, Noah, Abraham, Moses, and Jesus were great prophets.

There are two branches or styles of Islam—Sunni and Shi'ite. Sunnis believe anyone educated in Islam can become a religious leader. Shi'ites believe only descendants of Muhammad can be leaders.

Millions of Shi'ite Muslims make the pilgrimage to the Hussein Mosque in Karbala, Iraq, during Arba'een, a holiday that honors the martyrdom of Hussein bin Ali, the grandson of the Prophet Muhammad, and 72 followers in the Battle of Karbala.

Every year millions of Muslims make the pilgrimage to Mecca in Saudi Arabia. Called the hajj, it is the world's largest pilgrimage. Every healthy Muslim must do it at least once in his or her lifetime.

Here are a few other differences: Sunnis lower their heads to mats while praying. Shi'ites lower their heads on to hard clay. Sunnis believe Allah has a body and can sometimes be seen. Shi'ites believe Allah has no body and can't be seen. Sunnis believe Allah directly controls humans. Shi'ites believe Allah knows everything, but does not make people act a certain way.

Muslims follow religious rules called the Five Pillars of Islam. These include reciting the prayer known as *shahada:* "There is no god but Allah, and Muhammad is His messenger." Five times a day they face Mecca and pray; they have to give money to the poor; they have to fast (not eat) between sunrise and sunset during the Islamic holy month of Ramadan; and they must make at least one pilgrimage (trip) to Mecca. More than 2 million people make the trip, called the hajj, each year.[9]

Smoke and flames erupt from a gas chimney that is part of this Iranian gas and oil field near the town of Ahwaz in the Khuzestan province.

Oil and the Economy

Oil is big business in Iran, but not for ordinary citizens. Why? While the average person can own small businesses such as farms, stores, and workshops, only the government can run big businesses such as oil and natural gas. In fact, the government controls almost everything about the economy.[1] It determines the prices of goods rather than using the supply-and-demand method favored in the United States. Government pricing slows down economic growth, especially for private business.

One result of state-run businesses is a high rate of unemployment and underemployment. Many of Iran's educated youth are leaving the country to find jobs. When the best and brightest people take their talents to other countries, their native country suffers a "brain drain." This, in turn, slows business growth, and the cycle spirals downward.

Iran also has a lot of coal, magnesium ores, and gypsum. Farming is still important, but drought and the fact that more and more people are moving to the cities have caused food shortages.[2]

Wheat, rice, and barley are the major crops. Wheat is big in Iran because nearly everyone eats bread.[3] It is grown on irrigated lands, and on mountain slopes and plains. Rice is grown mostly in the wet Caspian lowlands in the north.

To generate electricity, Iran started a nuclear power program, which required producing nuclear fuel. That contributed to feelings of distrust between Iran and the United States. When Iran built its first atomic power station near the city of Bushehr, the United States government

Women sow rice in a field in the province of Mazandaran on the coast of the Caspian Sea. Rice is a vital crop in northern Iran.

Red poppies grow wild in the Zagros Mountains. Iran is one of the biggest producers of ornamental flowers in the world. Roses, tulips, fritillaria, poppies, and pittosporum are native to the country, but other species are grown as well. Roses, gerberas, tulips, Peruvian lilies (*Alsteromeria*), irises, chrysanthemums, and orchids are very popular among Iranians.[7]

accused Iran of trying to build nuclear weapons.[4] Iranian leaders insisted that it was making nuclear fuel for peaceful purposes only.[5] Still, in 2009 it tested missiles that could reach much of Europe. To get Iran to stop developing its nuclear technology, the United Nations (UN) imposed increasing sanctions designed to hurt the country's economy. The sanctions did not stop Iran from continuing its nuclear plans. Iranians have accused the United States of sending spies disguised as UN inspectors to check on its nuclear program.[6]

An Iranian woman weaves a large rug in the city of Esfahan. Persian rugs are considered among the world's best. Some museums, including those in Paris, London, and Austria, display these rugs just like they do great paintings.

Iranian Art and Music

Nasir Jallal offers a smile, tea, and salmon. The tea he made himself. The salmon came from friends who started as clients.

"It's good to see you, my friend," he says. Nasir doesn't shake a hand as much as embrace it. He gestures toward a table in the back of his Bloomington, Indiana, rug store that has briefly morphed into a mini café.

Nasir is a master weaver, appraiser, and repairer of oriental rugs that are more works of art than floor coverings. His carpets come from countries such as Afghanistan, Turkey, China, and India, but some of the best and most expensive ones come from Iran. People will spend thousands of dollars for one, sometimes $25,000 or more.

Why?

"People are so involved with art and when they see these rugs they can't take it," Nasir says. "The rugs talk to them. They bring out amazing feelings. They make a room very warm and welcoming."[1]

In Iran, carpet weavers have been praised for more than a thousand years. They combine intriguing patterns with vibrant colors, creating images of elegant patterns and designs, of flowers, plants, birds, and beasts, of real creatures and those of legend. The yarns are dyed using wildflowers in rich colors of burgundy, navy blue, and ivory. It is often washed in tea to soften the texture. A lot of carpets look like Persian gardens.[2]

Scientists believe farmers and people who raised cattle and sheep started carpet weaving on the plains of Iran. They used the wool from sheep to make yarn, and covered the floor with carpets rather than animal hides.

What is perhaps the world's oldest carpet, woven in the fifth century BCE, was discovered in 1949 near Mongolia. It is 9.3 feet by 6.5 feet (2.8 meters by 2 meters). Colors include dark red, green, blue, yellow, and pale orange. Images of a yellow spotted deer (which lived only near the shores of the Caspian Sea in northern Iran), a mythical winged creature, and a man on a horse are woven into the margins. It is preserved in the Hermitage Museum of Leningrad in Russia.[3]

Other traditional forms of art are calligraphy, painting, pottery, and music. Calligraphy is the art of fine handwriting, and in Iran it has reached a world-class level. Iranians used it to make distinctive copies of ancient manuscripts, especially of the Koran and the epic poem Shahnameh. They would also use it on pottery and historic buildings. Ancient Persians wrote letters and signs on dishes and cylinder seals.

Persian painters rank with the best in the ancient world. There are caves in Iran's Lorestan province that showcase images of animals and hunting scenes. Others in Fars province are at least 5,000 years old.

Iranian pottery (also called gombroon) started when ancient Persians first began farming around 4000 BCE.[4] They made forks and

Iranian potter Reza Ebadi puts the final touches on a piece at his workshop in Natanz, Iran.

knives out of clay. Pottery started as simple earthenware, usually in black or red. They gradually started decorating them with geometric designs. They also invented a pottery rotating machine to make bowls, jars, and pots. Archaeological sites are filled with pottery artifacts, and the occupation of a potter (*kuzeh gar*) is well documented in Persian literature. Even today, Iranian pottery is known for its quality.

Persian music has existed since ancient times. Musicians developed such instruments as the *ney* (Iranian flute) and the tambourine.[5] The *ney* is the oldest wind instrument. It is a tube made of cane with seven joints and six knots. Another Iranian

An Iranian man playing the *kamancheh*

wind instrument is the *soma,* which is like the oboe. It is usually accompanied by the *dohol* or *naghareb,* which are like drums. They are often played together during mourning ceremonies.

The *dohol* is a hollow cylinder-like drum with a diameter of around three feet (one meter) and a height of 10 to 12 inches (25 to 30 centimeters). Both ends of the cylinder are covered with tightly stretched skin. The *dohol* is played with two sticks: one is thick like a walking stick, and the other is thin like a twig.

The *kamancheh* is a stringed instrument like a violin that rests on the floor.[6] It is used nationally, but is especially popular among Turkmen and Turk tribes. Other stringed instruments are the *barbat,* which is like a harp with a big body and a short neck, and the *rabab,* which has a melon-shaped body with a long neck and a resting spike at the bottom.

serkeh

sib

somayeh

sekkeh

samanu

sir

senjed

somaq

sabzeh

Koran

This Haft-Sin (7S) table, decorated for the Iranian New Year holiday of Norwuz, has seven symbolic items starting with the letter s: *sabzeh* (for rebirth), *samanu* (wealth), *senjed* (love), *sir* (medicine), *sib* (beauty and health), *somaq* (sunrise), *serkeh* (age and patience). Sometimes *sekkeh* (prosperity and wealth) and *somayeh* (fertility) are also included.

Iran's biggest soccer star is Ali Karimi, who has been called the "Asian Maradona" because of his speed and skill. He was the captain of Iran's 2010 World Cup team. However, he angered Iranian officials because of his support for reform. He also was fined US$40,000 and briefly suspended from the national team for reportedly drinking water after a practice during Ramadan, the monthlong holy period when, from sunrise to sunset, Muslims are not allowed to eat or drink anything. He denied breaking Muslim law.[1]

Sports are very popular in Iran, and the most popular sport is soccer. Iran has qualified for three World Cups: 1978, 1998, and 2006. The 1998 World Cup was special to Iranians because that's when they won their only World Cup match: 2-1 against the United States. There had been a lot of talk before the match because the countries had not been friendly since the 1979 hostage crisis, but players on both sides were respectful and showed good sportsmanship.

Even though Iran does not have the best team in the world, people still go to watch. Tehran has eight major soccer stadiums. The biggest is Azadi (which means "freedom" in Persian) Stadium; it seats 100,000 and was built in 1971. The city of Tabriz has the 71,000-seat Yadegar e Emam Stadium, which was built in 1996. The city of Esfehan has the 50,000-seat Naghsh e Jahan Stadium, which was built in 2003. Another 50,000-seater is Shiraz Stadium in Shiraz, built in 2010.[2]

Azadi Stadium has hosted a number of major events, including the 1974 Asian Games. It is part of the Azadi Sports Complex, which includes a rowing river, a weightlifting center, swimming facilities, indoor volleyball courts, and other facilities.

Ali Karimi

Azadi Stadium is the world's fourth-biggest soccer stadium, third in Asia and first in the Middle East. Fans often get very excited during big matches, especially when the stadium gets filled beyond seating capacity. However, sometimes crowds can get aggressive. During the Iran-Japan World Cup qualifying match in 2005, seven people were killed in the stands.[3]

Iran is solid in basketball. It won the 2007 and 2010 Asian Games titles. However, Iran lost to the United States 88-51 at the 2010 World Championships in Turkey. Islamic law forbids public display of female skin, so during that game, U.S. cheerleaders covered up by wearing pants so as not to offend Iranian officials.[4]

Iranians have also had success in sports such as wrestling. It won four wrestling gold medals at the 2010 Asian Games.

Horses are raced at Park-e-Mellat in Tehran, and polo matches are played at the polo grounds on the Karadj Road out of Iran. Tennis instruction is available at the Amjadjeh Sports Center in Tehran. There are also golf courses in Tehran, plus several horseback riding clubs.

Iran is also known for its festivals. These festivals reflect the old and the new, and include the many cultures and religions that have become part of the region. Evident are Syrian and Roman influences, plus Persian culture and Zoroastrianism, the main religion in Persia before Islam became popular.

One of the most famous festivals is called Yalda (which means "birth"), or Shab-e Cheleh. It is celebrated in late December. Usually the longest night of the year, it was regarded as the night when evil was finally defeated and holy powers won the struggle for humans. It represents the victory of the Zoroastrian god Mazda over the demon Ahriman.

As with all Iranian festivals, food is very important during Yalda. Many of the recipes include melon, because melons are supposed to ward off illnesses. Cooks even put melon in pies and breads. Prayers are held throughout the day, and the celebration increases at night.

Jashn means "celebration," and Zoroastrians generally have a lot of fun at the Jashn-e-Sadeh (Festival of the Hundred) in January. It is held 100 days and nights (so 50 days) before the New Year. Families keep wood burning during the day. The flame is believed to chase away demons—the pure fire defeats "the forces of darkness, frost, and cold."[5] Visitors often share the small bonfires that burn on nearly every street in Tehran during this two- or three-day festival. Attending this festival is one of the best ways to get to know Iran's cultural heritage.

No Ruz (also Norwuz or Norouz) celebrates the Persian New Year. It comes during the spring equinox—the time when day and night are about the same length (the first day of spring). The major cultures of Mesopotamia have celebrated it for 5,000 years. In Iran, No Ruz can last for two weeks.[6]

There are also a number of Islamic holy days and other public holidays, most of which celebrate the life of Muhammad and his descendants. These include Arbaeen (honors the death of Muhammad's grandson), the Birth of Prophet Muhammad, the Death of Prophet Muhammad, and the Martyrdom of Iman Reza (a descendant of Muhammad).[7] Iran's version of the Fourth of July is called Republic Day. It honors the April 1979 Islamic Revolution.

 All ancient visitors had to pass through the Gate of Xerxes on their way to pay their respects to the Persian king.

We Visit Iran

Iranian history is apparent all across this diverse country—in the deserts, the plains, the mountains, and the cities. Ancient ruins dazzle even as they link a legendary past with a troubled present.

Imagine trudging under a broiling summer sun on a brown Iranian desert plain, a light blue sky above, bluish-white mountains looming in the distance, the ruins of a great capital spread all around you. You are in the southwestern Iranian province of Fars, about 35 miles (56 kilometers) northeast of the city of Shiraz.

The great Persian king Darius I, also known as Darius the Great, once ruled here. Legend says Alexander the Great torched the city after defeating the Persians. It might have been payback for earlier Persian invasions of Greece, or it might have been accidental. Nobody knows for sure.

You are a visitor to the most famous and popular site in Iran. Foreign visitors call this city Persepolis,[1] meaning "capital of Persia" in Greek. Iranians often refer to it as Takht-e Jamshid, which is Persian for "Throne of Jamshid." The ancient Persians called it Parsa. It was the summer capital of the Achaemenid kings who once ruled this land. At its peak, more than 29 nations would send representatives to the palace to pay respect to and attend meetings with the Persian emperors.

The huge palace complex took 150 years to finish. Darius the Great ordered construction to begin in 518 BCE on a half-artificial, half-natural terrace that was 1,475 feet (450 meters) long, 985 feet (300

meters) wide, and about 25 to 60 feet (8 to 18 meters) high. The palaces were given names. There was the huge Apadana, also known as the Audience Hall of Darius. East of that was the Throne Hall, which early archaeologists called the Hall of One Hundred Columns. Other buildings included the palaces of Darius and Xerxes and the royal treasury.

A double stairway of 106 steps about 23 feet (7 meters) wide led to the enormous Gate of Xerxes. The gateway has three doors and a hallway. The doors are covered with ancient inscriptions and carvings. There also are carvings of double-headed eagles.

South of the gateway is the Audience Hall, where kings met with visitors and celebrated Noruz (the Persian New Year). Nearby is the Central Hall, which has 36 stone columns each about 60 feet (20 meters) high. Double-headed bulls that represent ancient people decorate the stairways.

Just ahead is the Persepolis Museum, which now showcases ceramic works, carvings, cloths, and coins discovered in the area. Archaeologists are not sure whether the building was for Xerxes' harem (all his wives) or was the queen's palace.

Much of the wealth of the Persian Empire was stored in the treasury, which consisted of several buildings covering an area of more than 10,000 square feet (930 square meters). Scientists found stone and clay tablets written in the ancient languages of Akkadian and Elamite that gave details of daily life in Persepolis, including how much people made, the hours they worked, and vacations they took.

Kings were considered blessed by the god Ahuramazda (the Wise Lord, creator of heaven and earth) to build a great empire that would bring peace, order, and riches to the world. Darius the Great said, "It is not my will that the strong should oppress the weak. . . . God's plan is not turmoil but peace, prosperity, and good government."[2]

Darius backed up that belief. Persepolis was not built by slaves, but by workers who lived off site and who had a good lifestyle.

Nobody knows how many people lived there. It could have been anywhere from several thousand to tens of thousands. Generations of workers were born, lived, and died on the construction site.

There are other famous historical sites, some thousands of years old, some only a few hundred. Chogha Zanbil is a ziggurat that was built near Susa in 1250 BCE.[3] Millions of bricks were used in its construction. Some are engraved in cuneiform, an ancient form of writing. It is surrounded by three huge walls and can be seen from far away. The temple was never finished.

The ancient capital city of Pasargadae, built by the Achaemenians, shows the first examples of Persian garden planning and of Persian palaces.[4] The tomb of Cyrus the Great is there. This mausoleum was as famous then as the Lincoln Memorial is today. The ruins include a fortified terrace called Tall-e Takht, a gatehouse, an audience hall, a residential palace, and gardens.

The ancient desert city of Bam, on the southern edge of the Iranian high plateau, was founded around the same time as Pasargadae. It flourished from 700 CE to 1000 CE, when it was at the crossroads of many of the important trade routes that took such goods as silk and cotton garments from India and the Far East to Europe. The town was part of an oasis created by tapping into underground water. Underground canals, called qanats, were built. Bam has a citadel, which is a medieval fort that also served as a small town. It was built using mud brick layers and remained well preserved—its tan towers and walls looked almost golden in early mornings and late afternoons—until the 2003 earthquake destroyed most of it. Efforts to restore the citadel continued into 2011.[5]

Tehran was settled at least 8,000 years ago, perhaps more. People started building bazaars in the country around 6,000 years ago, and the largest one, the Grand Bazaar, is in Tehran.[6] Some of its corridors are more than 6 miles (10 kilometers) long. Each corridor in this huge marketplace specializes in selling certain goods, such as carpets (lots of carpets), copper, spices, paper, and art. Parts of the bazaar are enclosed and contain banks, investment businesses, mosques, and even hotels. A lot of it is open to the sky.

A bazaar in Shiraz, Iran

Tehran's 400-year-old Golestan Palace (Palace of Flowers) became the official home of the royal family.[7] In the twentieth century, it was used for royal receptions.

To the northwest is Tabriz, the country's second-largest city. It has a restored blue mosque that was built in 1465, and the covered Qaisariyeh Bazaar, which was started six hundred years ago.

Also in the northwest, about 14 miles (22 kilometers) from the great salt lake called Lake Oroumieh, is the town of Oroumieh. That town claims to be the birthplace of Zoroastrianism.

Another popular place is the Golden Triangle, an area in western Iran. It includes the ancient cities of Hamadan, Kermanshah, and

The city of Bam before an earthquake destroyed it in 2003

Khorramabad. This part of Iran was famous for the Silk Road, the path that traders used to take goods from the Far East, such as India and China, to the Middle East and Europe. This is part of the Iranian Plateau, and the terrain is rolling and diverse with mountains, rivers, and elevated flat land.

Hamadan was once a summer capital for the Persian emperors. It includes the Stone Lion monument, which dates back to the time of Alexander the Great. Near Kermanshah are the Tagh-e Bostan grottoes, caves that have been carved with bas-relief sculptures. They were made by chipping away at slabs of rock to make pictures stand out. The Persians, along with the Egyptians and Greeks, were famous for this type of artwork.

Esfahan, or Isfahan, which is located in the central part of Iran, is the former capital of Persia. The city has a huge tree-covered central square that has spectacular monuments on all four sides. It features two mosques, a fifteenth-century palace, gardens, and a bazaar. The Friday Mosque (Masjid-e Jomeh) is one of the finest buildings in Iran. The mosque Sheikh Lotfullah is famous for its unique front entrance.

This bas-relief sculpture at Tagh-e Bostan shows Shapur II (309–379 CE) being named king of Persia. Shapur was the first king to order the rock carvings in these caves.

The holy shrine of Hazrat-e Masumeh in the holy city of Qom is as important to Shi'ite Muslims as Vatican City is to Roman Catholics.

Built by Shah Abbas the Great at the beginning of the seventeenth century, the mosque Sheikh Lotfullah is a great example of Iranian architecture.

The province of Khorasan, located in the northeastern part of the country, is where a great revival of learning occurred during the Middle Ages. The town of Mashad, which was once a trading post on the Silk Road, is the capital of the region.

To understand Iran, one should understand how its past shapes its future. It is a nation of contrasts that cannot be ignored. It is a country of oil wealth and yearning youth, of growing power and mounting unrest; it defies outside influence, especially from the United States. It has the Middle East's longest-lasting democratic movement despite an iron-fisted religious government that suppresses opposition, even as it allows democracy to survive. It is a country that mirrors its geography—rich, diverse, and always fascinating.

Iranian Kabab Kubideh

Also known as *kabab koobideh,* it is served for dinner. Some Persian restaurants serve it with *kabab barg* and call it *Soltani,* which means "Sultan's Feast." These kababs are cooked on a grill, so be sure to work under adult supervision.

Ingredients
1 pound ground beef or lamb
1 medium onion, grated
¼ cup bread crumbs or white flour
1 egg, slightly beaten
1 teaspoon tumeric
1 teaspoon salt
½ teaspoon pepper
1 Tablespoon lemon juice

Directions
1. In order to prevent the mix from falling off the skewers, drain the water (juice) out of the grated onion. Mix all ingredients well. Cover and leave in refrigerator overnight or for a few hours. The colder the mix, the better it will stick to the skewers.
2. Divide the meat into 10 to 12 portions. Press each portion around a long metal skewer and shape it evenly.
3. Place the skewers a few inches away from the grill coals. Turn constantly for a couple of minutes and then cook each side for a few minutes. Serve with rice.

Persian designs can be used for a lot of art projects, from rugs to embroidery to stained glass or tiling. Here's how to make your own design:

Materials
Persian rug shop or web sites that feature Persian rugs
Colored pencils
Drawing paper
Graph paper

1. Look at actual rugs, either in shops or in photos or even on web sites such as Pak Persian Rugs. They are divided into categories based on their patterns—rectilinear (which means they have angles and straight lines), curvilinear (curved or rounded lines), or both. Most Persian rug designs usually have a medallion at the center surrounded by a repeated theme or pattern. The most common Persian rug design patterns are diamonds, squares, triangles, hexagons, stars, crosses, and stripes. There also are curved images of trees, such as a tree of life that shows birds, chickens, fish, fruit, and flowers. Other ideas for curved images are jugs, flower-filled vases, leaves, dogs, and flames.
2. Decide what materials and colors you'll use. Look at the area where you'll display the project to help you decide on the best colors and on how difficult to make your pattern.
3. Draw your ideas on paper using colored pencils. When you are happy with your design, draw it to scale on graph paper.
4. Take the drawing to the area where the rug will be displayed to make sure everything matches and looks good. Make changes as needed.

TIMELINE

BCE

1600	Aryan tribes move into what is now Iran.
550	Cyrus the Great begins to build what becomes the Persian Empire.
331	Alexander the Great conquers Persia and most of the Middle East.

CE

640	Arab invasion ends Sassanian dynasty and starts Islamic rule.
1220	Genghis Khan leads Mongol invasion of the area.
1921	Military commander Reza Khan seizes power in February.
1925	In December, Parliament votes to make Reza Khan ruler.
1935	Formerly known as Persia, *Iran* is adopted as the country's official name.
1941	The shah's support of Germany and Italy in World War II leads to the U.S.-Britain-Russian occupation of Iran. The shah is removed in favor of his son, Mohammad Reza Pahlavi.
1950	Ali Razmara becomes prime minister and is assassinated less than nine months later. He is succeeded by the nationalist Mohammad Mossadeq.
1953	In August, Mossadeq is overthrown in a coup engineered by Great Britain and the United States. General Fazlollah Zahedi is proclaimed as prime minister, and the shah returns.
1963	The shah campaigns to modernize and westernize the country.
1978	The shah's policies alienate the clergy. His authoritarian rule leads to riots, strikes, and mass demonstrations. Martial law is imposed.
1979	In January, the shah and his family are forced into exile. On February 1, the Islamic fundamentalist Ayatollah Ruhollah Khomeini returns to Iran following 14 years of exile in Iraq and France for opposing the regime. On April 1, the Islamic Republic of Iran is proclaimed. Seven months later, Islamic militants take 63 Americans hostage inside the U.S. Embassy in Tehran. They demand the return of the shah, who is in the United States for medical treatment.
1980	The exiled shah dies of cancer in Egypt. On September 22 the Iran-Iraq war begins.
1981	The American hostages are released in January, ending 444 days in captivity.
1988	Iran accepts a cease-fire agreement with Iraq.
1989	Khomeini dies on June 3. The next day, President Khamene'i is appointed as new supreme leader.
1995	The United States imposes oil and trade sanctions over Iran's alleged sponsorship of terrorism, seeking to acquire nuclear arms, and hostility to the Middle East peace process.
2002	U.S. President George W. Bush describes Iraq, Iran, and North Korea as an "axis of evil." The speech causes outrage in Iran.
2004	Conservatives regain control of parliament in February elections. Before the polls, thousands of reformist candidates are disqualified. In June, the United Nations rebukes Iran for failing to fully cooperate with an inquiry into its nuclear activities.
2005	Mahmoud Ahmadinejad wins the presidential election.
2009	Ahmadinejad is declared to have won a reelection. Rival candidates allege vote-rigging. Violence follows, and hundreds of journalists are jailed. In September, Iran test-fires a series of medium- and long-range missiles that put Israel and U.S. bases in the Persian Gulf within striking range.
2010	UN Security Council increases sanctions against Iran over its nuclear program. Sarah Shourd, one of three U.S. citizens detained for spying when they were hiking too close to the Iran-Iraq border, is freed after a year in prison. The three deny they were spying.
2011	President Ahmadinejad survives feud with Supreme Leader Ayatollah Ali Khamenei.

Introduction

1. CIA *World Fact Book,* "Iran," https://www.cia.gov/library/publications/the-world-factbook/geos/ir.html
2. *iExplore:* "Iran Travel Guide, Iran Overview," http://www.iexplore.com/dmap/Iran/Overview&nav=next
3. Anousheh Ansari. "First Female Private Space Explorer and First Space Ambassador," 2009, http://www.anoushehansari.com/about/
4. *iExplore:* "Iran Travel Guide, Where to Go in Iran," http://www.iexplore.com/dmap/Iran/Where+to+Go

Chapter 1. Welcome to Iran

1. *iExplore:* "Iran Travel Guide, Iran Overview." http://www.iexplore.com/dmap/Iran/Overview&nav=next
2. *iExplore:* "Iran Travel Guide, Where to Go in Iran," http://www.iexplore.com/dmap/Iran/Where+to+Go
3. Simon Tisdall, "Embassy Cable Tells of Elderly American's Escape from Iran," *The Guardian,* November 28, 2010, http://www.guardian.co.uk/world/2010/nov/28/american-escape-iran-horse-turkey
4. Brett Michael Dykes. "WikiLeaks Cable Depicts American's Harrowing Escape from Iran on Horseback," *Yahoo! News,* November 29, 2010, http://news.yahoo.com/s/yblog_thelookout/20101129/ts_yblog_thelookout/wikileaks-cable-reveals-daring-horseback-escape-from-iran-by-u-s-dentist
5. David E. Sanger, "The Larger Game in the Middle East—Iran," *The New York Times,* April 2, 2011. http://www.nytimes.com/2011/04/03/weekinreview/03sanger.html

Chapter 2. History of Iran

1. Editors Time-Life Books, *TimeFrame 600–400 BC, A Soaring Spirit* (New York: Time-Life Books Inc., 1987), pp. 14–22.
2. Ibid.
3. Stephen Kinzer, *All the Shah's Men* (Hoboken, N.J.: John Wiley & Sons, 2003), pp. 50–52.

Chapter 3. Supreme Leader, Government of Faith

1. Imam Khomeini's Biography, http://imam-khomeini.com/ShowItem.aspx?id=11653&cat=11460&lang=en

2. *iExplore:* "Iran Travel Guide, Where to Go in Iran," http://www.iexplore.com/dmap/Iran/Where+to+Go
3. Lawrence K. Altman, "Dr. Jean A. Bernard, 98, Dies; Found Cancer in Shah of Iran," *The New York Times,* April 30, 2006. http://www.nytimes.com/2006/04/30/world/europe/30bernard.html
4. CIA *World Fact Book,* "Iran," https://www.cia.gov/library/publications/the-world-factbook/geos/ir.html
5. Ibid.
6. *BBC News:* Country Profiles, "Iran," http://news.bbc.co.uk/2/hi/europe/country_profiles/790877.stm
7. Ibid.
8. "Iran: Mir Hossein Mousavi and Mehdi Karroubi 'arrested,' " *BBC News,* February 28, 2011. http://www.bbc.co.uk/news/world-middle-east-12599837

Chapter 4. A Land to Explore

1. NASA Earth Observatory: "Mt. Damavand, Iran," http://earthobservatory.nasa.gov/IOTD/view.php?id=5267
2. Araz Advanture Tours: "Mt. Damavand," http://www.araz.org/tours/Programs%20details/Damavand.htm
3. *iExplore:* "Iran Travel Guide, Overview" http://www.iexplore.com/dmap/Iran/Overview&nav=next
4. *iExplore:* "Iran Travel Guide, Where to Go in Iran," http://www.iexplore.com/dmap/Iran/Where+to+Go
5. Iran Tourism and Touring Online: "Persian Gulf Coast," http://www.itto.org/tourismattractions/?sight=599
6. "Iran's Lake Orumieh Shrinks Dramatically," *PressTV,* June 8, 2009, http://www.presstv.ir/detail/97415.html

Chapter 5. Everyday Life

1. CIA *World Fact Book,* "Iran," https://www.cia.gov/library/publications/the-world-factbook/geos/ir.html
2. *iExplore:* "Iran Travel Guide, Iran Food and Dining," http://www.iexplore.com/dmap/Iran/Dining;$sessionid$XTQCJ5QAAEIBUP2MN5XCFEQ
3. Iranian Cultural and Information Center, http://www.persia.org/

4. *BBC News:* Country Profiles, "Iran," http://news.bbc.co.uk/2/hi/europe/country_profiles/790877.stm

5. Embassy of the United States, "Press Release on World Press Freedom Prize to Iranian Journalist," April 8, 2011, http://uspolicy.be/headline/press-release-world-press-freedom-prize-iranian-journalist

6. Sean Alfano, "Shahla Jahed, Mistress of Iranian Soccer Star Nasser Mohammad Khani, Hanged for Murder in Tehran," *New York Daily News,* December 1, 2010, http://articles.nydailynews.com/2010-12-01/news/27083003_1_mistress-tehran-soccer

7. *iExplore:* "Iran Travel Guide, Where to Go in Iran," http://www.iexplore.com/dmap/Iran/Where+to+Go

8. "Green Wave, Green People," *Tehran Live,* June 8, 2009, http://tehranlive.org/2009/06/08/green-wavegreen-people/

9. Sacred Sites: Mecca, http://sacredsites.com/middle_east/saudi_arabia/mecca.html

Chapter 6. Oil and the Economy

1. CIA *World Fact Book,* "Iran," https://www.cia.gov/library/publications/the-world-factbook/geos/ir.html

2. *iExplore:* "Iran Travel Guide, Where to Go in Iran," http://www.iexplore.com/dmap/Iran/Where+to+Go

3. *Country Studies:* "Iranian Crops," U.S. Library of Congress, http://countrystudies.us/iran/76.htm

4. *BBC News:* Country Profiles, "Iran," http://news.bbc.co.uk/2/hi/europe/country_profiles/790877.stm

5. David E. Sanger, "The Larger Game in the Middle East—Iran," *The New York Times,* April 2, 2011, http://www.nytimes.com/2011/04/03/weekinreview/03sanger.html

6. Ali Akbar Dareini, "Iran Says UN Agency Sending Spies, Not Inspectors," *Associated Press,* December 4, 2010.

7. The Flower Expert: "National, Native and Popular Flower of Iran," http://www.theflowerexpert.com/content/flowerbusiness/flowergrowersandsellers/national-native-popular-flowers-of-iran

Chapter 7. Iranian Art and Music

1. Author interview with Nasir Jallal, August, 2010.

2. Iranian Cultural and Information Center, http://www.persia.org/

3. "The Pearl Carpet of Baroda," *Internet Stones.com,* http://www.internetstones.com/pearl-carpet-of-baroda-rectangular-shaped-deer-hyde-silk-glass-beads-pearls.html

4. Victor Epand, "The World of Iranian Pottery," February 12, 2008, http://ezinearticles.com/?The-World-Of-Iranian-Pottery&id=981815

5. Peyman Nasehpour, "Persian Musical Instruments," http://nasehpour.tripod.com/peyman/id47.html

6. "Persian Music," *Best Iran Travel,* http://www.bestirantravel.com/culture/music.html

Chapter 8. Sports and Festivals

1. Daniel Bettini, "Iranian Opposition Looks to Soccer Champ," Israel Culture, *Ynet News.com,* August 26, 2010, http://www.ynetnews.com/articles/0,7340,L-3943660,00.html

2. World Stadiums, "Stadiums in Iran," http://www.worldstadiums.com/middle_east/countries/iran.shtml

3. Soccer Stadiums, http://www.skyscrapercity.com/showthread.php?t=303110

4. Alexandra Sandels, "Cheerleaders Go For Modesty at Iran-U.S. Basketball Game," *Los Angeles Times,* September 2, 2010, http://latimesblogs.latimes.com/babylonbeyond/2010/09/turkey-iran-us-cheerleaders-basketball-hijab-.html

5. Fareydoon Tarapour, "Jashn-e-Sadeh, the Festival of Fire." *PressTV,* January 30, 2011, http://www.presstv.ir/detail/162750.html

6. Iranian Festivals, http://www.world66.com/asia/middleeast/iran/festivals

7. *iExplore:* "Iran Travel Guide, Iran Country and Tourist Information," http://www.iexplore.com/dmap/Iran/The+Essential

Chapter 9. We Visit Iran

1. Iranian Tours, "Persepolis," http://www.iraniantours.com/attractions/shiraz/pers.htm

2. Ibid.
3. Iran Tourist Attractions: "UNESCO Sites," http://www.destinationiran.com/unesco-list
4. Kwintessential: "Top Tourist Attractions, Iran" http://www.kwintessential.co.uk/articles/article/Iran/Top-Tourist-Attractions-Iran/129

5. *iExplore:* "Iran Travel Guide, Where to Go in Iran," http://www.iexplore.com/dmap/Iran/Where+to+Go
6. Iranian Tours: "Grand Bazaar, Tehran," http://www.iraniantours.com/attractions/tehran/bazaar.htm
7. Iranian Tours: "Golestan Palace," http://www.iraniantours.com/attractions/tehran/golestan.htm

FURTHER READING

Books

Bowden, Mark. *Guests of the Ayatollah, The Iranian Hostage Crisis.* New York: Grove Press, 2006.

Graham, Amy. *Iran in the News.* Berkeley Heights, NJ: Enslow Publishers, 2006.

Gray, Leon, Edmund Herziq, Dorreh Mirheydar. *National Geographic Countries of the World: Iran.* New York: National Geographic Society, 2008.

Kahlman, Bobbie. *Iran the Land.* New York: Crabtree Publishing, 2010.

McElwee, William. *Tales of Persia: Missionary Stories from Islamic Iran.* Phillipsburg, NY: P & R Publishing, 2005.

Richter, Joanne. *Iran the Culture.* New York: Crabtree Publishing, 2010.

Works Consulted

This book is based on the author's interview with Afghan-American Nasir Jallal in August 2010 and on the following sources:

Alfano, Sean. "Shahla Jahed, Mistress of Iranian Soccer Star Nasser Mohammad Khani, Hanged for Murder in Tehran." *New York Daily News,* December 1, 2010.

Dareini, Ali Akbar, "Iran Says UN Agency Sending Spies, Not Inspectors." *Associated Press,* December 4, 2010.

Altman, Lawrence K. "Dr. Jean A. Bernard, 98, Dies; Found Cancer in Shah of Iran." *The New York Times,* April 30, 2006.

Ansari, Anousheh. "First Female Private Space Explorer and First Space Ambassador." 2009. http://www.anoushehansari.com/about/

Araz Adventure Tours: "Mt. Damavand" http://www.araz.org/tours/Programs%20details/Damavand.htm

BBC News—Profile: Mahmoud Ahmadinejad http://www.bbc.co.uk/news/world-middle-east-10866448

Bettini, Daniel. "Iranian Opposition Looks to Soccer Champ," Israel Culture, *Ynet News.com,* August 26, 2010.

CIA *World Factbook.* "Iran." https://www.cia.gov/library/publications/the-world-factbook/geos/ir.html

Country Studies: "Iranian Crops," U.S. Library of Congress, http://countrystudies.us/iran/76.htm

Dabashi, Hamid. *Iran, A People Interrupted.* New York: The New Press, 2007.

Dykes, Brett Michael. "WikiLeaks Cable Depicts American's Harrowing Escape from Iran on Horseback." *Yahoo! News,* November 29, 2010.

Editors Time-Life Books. *TimeFrame 600–400 BC, A Soaring Spirit.* New York: Time-Life Books Inc., 1987.

Embassy of the United States. "Press Release on World Press Freedom Prize to Iranian Journalist." April 8, 2011.

Epand, Victor. "The World of Iranian Pottery." February 12, 2008. http://ezinearticles.com/?The-World-Of-Iranian-Pottery&id=981815

The Flower Expert: "National, Native and Popular Flower of Iran," http://www.theflowerexpert.com/content/flowerbusiness/flowergrowersandsellers/national-native-popular-flowers-of-iran

"Green Wave, Green People," *Tehran Live,* June 8, 2009.

Hourami, Albert. *A History of the Arab People.* New York: Grand Central Publishing, 1991.

Iran Online: Ancient Persian Festivals http://www.iranonline.com/festivals/

Iran Tourism and Touring Online: "Persian Gulf Coast" http://www.itto.org/tourismattractions/?sight=599

"Iran: Mir Hossein Mousavi and Mehdi Karroubi 'arrested,' " *BBC News,* February 28, 2011.

Iranian Festivals, http://www.world66.com/asia/middleeast/iran/festivals

"Iran's Lake Orumieh Shrinks Dramatically." *PressTV,* June 8, 2009.

Kennedy, Hugh. *The Great Arab Conquests: How the Spread of Islam Changed the World We Live In.* Philadelphia: DaCapo Press, 2008.

Kinzer, Stephen. *All the Shah's Men: An American Coup and the Roots of Middle East Terror.* Hoboken, NJ: John Wiley & Sons, 2008.

Kwintessential: "Top Tourist Attractions, Iran" http://www.kwintessential.co.uk/articles/article/Iran/Top-Tourist-Attractions-Iran/129

Lewis, Bernard. *The Middle East.* New York: Scribner, 1997.

Mackey, Sandra. *The Iranians. Persia, Islam and the Soul of a Nation.* London: Plume Penguin Group, 1998.

NASA Earth Observatory: "Mt. Damavand, Iran" http://earthobservatory.nasa.gov/IOTD/view.php?id=5267

"The Pearl Carpet of Baroda," *Internet Stones.com.* http://www.internetstones.com/pearl-carpet-of-baroda-rectangular-shaped-deer-hyde-silk-glass-beads-pearls.html

"Persian Greco-Roman Wrestlers Claim 2 More Asian Golds." *Payvand News Agency,* November 22, 2010. http://www.payvand.com/news/10/nov/1224.html

"Persian Music," *Best Iran Travel.* http://www.bestirantravel.com/culture/music.html

Peyman Nasehpour, "Persian Musical Instruments." http://nasehpour.tripod.com/peyman/id47.html

Sacred Sites: Mecca, http://sacredsites.com/middle_east/saudi_arabia/mecca.html

Sandels, Alexandra. "Cheerleaders Go For Modesty at Iran-U.S. Basketball Game," *Los Angeles Times,* September 2, 2010.

Sanger, David E. "The Larger Game in the Middle East—Iran." *The New York Times,* April 2, 2011.

Sciolino, Elaine. *Persian Mirrors, The Elusive Face of Iran.* New York: Free Press, Simon & Schuster Inc., 2005.

Tarapour, Fareydoon. "Jashn-e-Sadeh, the Festival of Fire." *PressTV,* January 30, 2011.

Tisdall, Simon. "Embassy Cable Tells of Elderly American's Escape from Iran." *The Guardian,* November 28, 2010.

World Stadiums: "Stadiums in Iran" http://www.worldstadiums.com/middle_east/countries/iran.shtml

On the Internet

BBC News: Country Profiles. "Iran" http://news.bbc.co.uk/2/hi/europe/country_profiles/790877.stm

Destination Iran http://www.destinationiran.com

Iranian Cultural and Information Center http://www.persia.org/

Iranian Tours http://www.iraniantours.com/

Iran Online http://www.iranonline.com

Iran Travel Guide http://www.iexplore.com/dmap/Iran/Overview&nav=next

U.S. Department of State: Iran http://travel.state.gov/travel/cis_pa_tw/cis/cis_1142.html

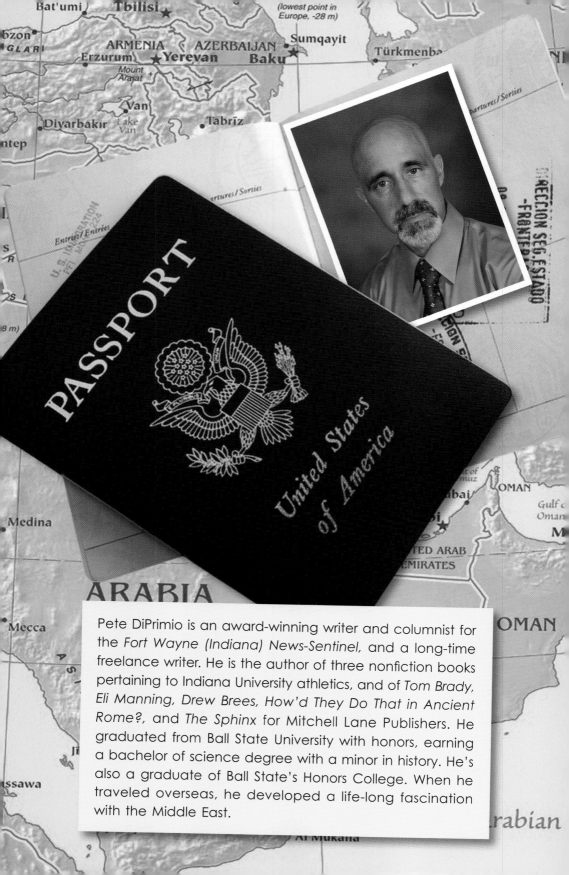

Pete DiPrimio is an award-winning writer and columnist for the *Fort Wayne (Indiana) News-Sentinel*, and a long-time freelance writer. He is the author of three nonfiction books pertaining to Indiana University athletics, and of *Tom Brady, Eli Manning, Drew Brees, How'd They Do That in Ancient Rome?*, and *The Sphinx* for Mitchell Lane Publishers. He graduated from Ball State University with honors, earning a bachelor of science degree with a minor in history. He's also a graduate of Ball State's Honors College. When he traveled overseas, he developed a life-long fascination with the Middle East.